Summary

Land privatization is traditionally accomplished through sequential steps. The first step usually focuses on developing an understanding of the linkages between private property rights and economic growth. In Mongolia, it is clear that this knowledge exists. What is still inadequate is the second step in the process—developing a sound and consistent policy (coupled with legislation and practical regulatory framework supporting that policy) for the development of private property rights.

Property rights and land privatization are at the forefront of economic growth, good governance, and urban/rural development in Mongolia. Many of the foundations for economic growth and income generation are necessarily based on sound land reform, private ownership, and secure property rights. Mongolia has been pursuing a deliberate and constructive program of property rights reform. However, in some ways, an urgency to address land and property rights reform has not been present in the country, due to in large part to its large size, small population, and historically singular focus on livestock production and common pool resources. Recent Government of Mongolia (GoM) efforts to develop new land and land privatization laws, while welcome, fall short of a policy and practical regulatory framework needed to realize the benefits of land privatization (increased capital formation, social stability, greater sustainable resource use, and reduced corruption/improved governance).

USAID has been at the forefront of land reform efforts worldwide. Based specifically upon lessons learned in more than a dozen former Soviet Union (FSU) countries, USAID/Mongolia should focus, now, on providing support to property rights policy reform and supportive legislative and regulatory development.

During a recent scoping exercise conducted by USAID specialists in land tenure and property rights (November 16-24, 2004), a host of property rights issues and concerns were identified. These are broadly noted in this paper. There are, however, three major issues regarding property rights and land privatization in the country that USAID should address. These are:

1. **Property Rights Policy** – There is an important need to consolidate and develop a comprehensive land and property rights policy framework in Mongolia. Present efforts, while important, are happening in a poorly coordinated and inadequately informed manner. USAID is importantly placed to galvanize government and lead donor efforts in the development of land and property rights policy.

2. **Legal Framework** – Land laws are generally well intentioned but address land, property rights, and natural resources management in a disjointed fashion. Several of the 2002 and 2003 land laws can be seen as important tools, but are already outdated and in need of either revision and/or a strong and practical regulatory framework to secure their implementation. The absence of clear property rights is undermining investment, contributing to corruption, and undermining economic development. Laws are needed to confirm property rights and implement a private property rights policy framework.

3. **Education and Training** – Much of the policy and legal framework for land and property rights is evolving within a limited understanding of their role in national economic growth and development. This is particularly the case for (recently elected) legislators and the legal profession. In addition, judges, *aimag* and *soum* administrators, and adjudicators, etc. are all expected to implement land laws on which they have limited knowledge and familiarity. Basic land law and property rights education is urgently needed to steer the development and implementation of new legislation and regulations. In addition, a set of functional and strategic land reform concepts is necessary to engage decision makers in policy-level discussions.

1.0 Background

Over the past three decades, USAID and its partners have learned a great deal about the relationship between property rights, economic growth, democracy, governance, natural resource management, and conflict. In recent years, a number of donors have engaged in reviews of experience and comparative analyses of land tenure policy in order to understand lessons learned and to shape a new land policy consensus.[1] Still, there is ongoing need to understand (1) how land tenure relations shift as societies move through various stages of democratization, economic growth, and in some cases from war to peace; and (2) how these shifts require different property rights regimes (and sequencing) that will lead to further economic growth, sustainable resource management, and political stability.

Lack of secure and negotiable property rights is critical to economic development and social stability. In countries where USAID has provided support to strengthen property rights, there have been measurable successes in economic investment and growth, transition to democratic government, and improved use of resources. Two important lessons have been learned from the past decade of research and policy work:

♦ Property rights and institutions that are inconsistent with economic, political, and environmental realities can undermine growth, erode sustainable resources management, and promote violent conflict. Conversely, property rights systems that are viewed as legitimate, transparent, and negotiable, lead to increased investment, political stability, and sustainable resource use.

♦ There is an appropriate sequence of reforms that will lead to stronger, more robust, and efficient property rights systems. Reforms, policies, or activities that are introduced out of sequence can lead to under-investment, resource misuse, and degradation—or worse, violent conflict among property owners or users.[2]

Land is the ultimate resource and is both a physical commodity as well as an abstract concept related to the rights to own or to use it. Land tenure is the institutional (political, economic, social, and legal) structure that determines how individuals and groups secure access to the productive capabilities of the land. Land management is the process through which land resources are utilized, while land administration addresses issues related to land information and how they can be utilized for effective and efficient land management.

The basic issues of land tenure, property rights, and natural resource management are concerned with questions of access to resources, the distribution of resources to members of the society, and the security of tenure that these members of society hold over these resources. Other issues or problems, such as conflict over land, landlessness and inequitable land distribution, institutional or legal reform, land markets, and natural resource management, derive from these basic issues:

Access to land addresses issues related to how people are able to enter onto and utilize a physically defined area of land. Access rights are defined in terms of location, time, use, and the individual's relation to the community and the state. Where is the land located relative to other land; how long can it be used;

---

[1] See in particular the World Bank Policy Research Review on Land Issues.
[2] For example, programs for individualization and titling of land parcels may be undertaken that undermine group ownership and common property management, where the cost of maintaining individual titles outweighs the benefits, or where benefits are negligible because distorted factor markets discourage investment or productive land use.

what types of uses are permitted; and how do individual rights relate to those of the community or nation are all factors addressed in questions of access to land.

Distribution of property rights refers to how these rights are allocated to different members of a society. Are land rights concentrated in the hands of a few people or groups of the society while the majority of people have little or no land rights (is 80% of the land controlled by 5% of the population)? Do certain minorities have limited access to land in comparison to other groups, or is high-value land (rather than large amounts of land) concentrated in the hands of a few people?

Security of tenure refers to the institutional or social mechanisms that ensure that a land user will have continued access to a given piece of land. Security of tenure may be related to a community-recognized and socially sanctioned right for that individual to use the land or it may be more formal in terms of lease or title documents. The security is derived from the ability of the individual to enforce or ensure his/her right of continued access to the land. Insecurity of tenure would conversely imply that there are few mechanisms available to the individual to protect his/her land and property rights.

An understanding of these basic relationships permits a further categorization of property rights issues. The political, economic, and social structures in a given society have a further impact on these relationships. Thus, issues of immediate concern will vary depending on the level of stability in the country, the historic distribution of landholdings, institutional structures in place to protect property rights, the ability to make property transactions, and, ultimately, the sustainable utilization of land and other natural resources.

The understanding of these relationships also assists in the development of possible policy and program interventions to address areas of concern. These interventions may address questions of good governance; conflict resolution; the institutional, legal, and regulatory framework; resource redistribution; land administration and management; and land use planning and conservation. More specifically in a situation of conflict and instability, policy interventions might address issues related to dispute resolution or the identification of land for the settlement of refugees. Inadequacies or inequalities in land distribution might be addressed through programs for the allocation of state land or through redistribution as part of land reform. Insecure land and property rights might be addressed through institutional reform, land registration program, or law reform initiatives. Poorly performing property markets might be addressed through the collection and provision of readily accessible public market information, training of real estate professionals, or reform in the financial sector. Examples of financial sector reform have typically included land as collateral, the consolidation of land and immovable property as collateral, and the development of mortgage (writ. land) markets. Unsustainable natural resource management might be addressed through more secure property rights for resource user groups, forestation/reforestation investments and programs, programs for community participation in protected areas management, or tax incentives for improved conservation practices. The design of the possible interventions will vary from one country to another and is dependent on the political will, opportunities, and resources available.

1.1 USAID, Land Reform and Property Rights in the Former Soviet Union: Lessons Learned

There have been successful land and property rights reforms in the former Soviet Union (FSU). USAID has facilitated the privatization of property rights in Russia, Ukraine, Moldova, Albania, Georgia, and Kyrgyzstan, and is improving the legal framework for property rights in Kazakhstan, Tajikistan, and Uzbekistan. In Ukraine, where USAID has privatized several million parcels and supervised the distribution of over 3 million land titles, the country has witnessed a fundamental shift in economic and social conditions. Land markets, while not completely free (private transactions are scheduled to be legalized in 2005), have emerged from leasehold rights. Hundreds of thousands of legal land transactions are taking place there. Private commercial farms have emerged, leased-in land, secured loans, and measurably increased production and shareholder wealth. Household producers have seen increases in household wealth as well, as they capitalize on opportunities to engage in production of high-value crops or lease-out land to commercial producers. Urban property sales and the establishment of land taxes have provided financing for municipal development. In Moldova, where USAID also facilitated privatization of agricultural and urban land, similar outcomes have been witnessed. More than 75% of commercial farms operating have leased-in land. Market-led land consolidation is taking place, and smaller, uneconomic landholders now have the option of opting out of agriculture by selling or leasing their land. In Kyrgyzstan, (a country like Mongolia with a significant percentage of the population engaged in herding), USAID assisted with the development of laws and legislation to privatize agricultural and other rural land uses. In the last few years, as the privatization of land has taken hold, more than 50% of farming operations have experienced significant economic growth, while another 25% are on the road to growth. Urban land sales have contributed to the funding of municipal budgets. Thus, it has become increasingly evident that, in a relatively short period of time, secure property rights have been critical to the development of wealth in post-Soviet economic development.

2.0 A Framework for Analyzing Land Reform, Property Rights, and Land Privatization in Mongolia

Between November 16 and 24, 2004, two Land Tenure and Property Rights Specialists (Dr. Gregory Myers and Mr. Peter E. Hetz) visited Mongolia at the request of the USAID Mission to Mongolia. The purpose of their trip was to examine recent efforts aimed at land reform and, in particular, at land privatization in Mongolia and to identify issues arising. During their brief visit, they visited with USAID and U.S Embassy staff. In addition, they conducted 18 meetings with GoM officials, USAID contractors, donors/donor programs, and civil society. A list of meetings can be found in Appendix A.

Though brief, their investigations focused on land privatization within the context of a conceptual framework for land tenure and property rights that is being developed by USAID for this purpose. The team used the categorization of issues in this framework and the set of policy and programming interventions to examine land reform issues to date in Mongolia.

2.1 Land and Property Rights Issues

The following categories are used to characterize general land and property rights issues:

- *Conflict/Instability*, including instability and lack of governance in post-conflict situations, or conflict that arises in the course of economic, social, or institutional change.
- *Landlessness or Inequitable Land Distribution*, including landlessness, inequitable land distribution, and insufficient access to land and related natural resources to secure livelihoods.
- *Insecure Land and Property Rights*, including insecure property rights in land and property that create conflict, undermine economic incentives and investments, and constrain property transfers.
- *Poorly Performing Land Markets*, including incomplete tenure forms, market failures, or a land market that is highly segmented due to constrained access by the poor, ethnicity, and/or lack of tenure security.
- *Unsustainable Natural Resources Management*, including deforestation, land degradation, and unsustainable use of land, water, forests, and pasture due to conflict/instability, landlessness, insecure land and property rights, or poorly performing land markets.

2.2 Policy and Program Interventions

The rows in Table1 reflect common (and usually crosscutting) policy and program interventions generically targeted to address land issue constraints:

- *Good Governance* beginning with the precondition of political will and pursuit of democratic governance aimed at establishing and/or restoring rule of law. Also includes general public information and education.
- *Conflict or Dispute Resolution,* including both formal and alternative dispute resolution methods and strengthening recourse to the rule of law.
- *Institutions (Legal and Regulatory Framework)* including creation of property institutions, both for individual and communally held property, and for rural and urban uses, that secure rights of ownership, transferability, exclusiveness, and use.
- *Redistribution*, including land, pasture and agrarian reform, resettlement, farm restructuring, and privatization.

❑ *Land Administration*, including efficiency improvements in the functioning of land administration systems along with decentralization and devolution.
❑ *Land Use Planning and Conservation*, including zoning, urban and regional planning, common pool resources management, and buffer zone and protected area management.

Table 1   A Conceptual Framework for Land Tenure and Property Rights Reform

		LAND AND PROPERTY RIGHTS ISSUES CATEGORIZATION				
		Conflict/ Instability	Insecure Land and Property Rights	Landlessness /Inequitable Land Distribution	Poorly Performing Land Markets	Unsustainable Natural Resource Management
LTPR POLICY AND PROGRAM INTERVENTIONS	Good Governance					
	Conflict or Dispute Resolution					
	Institutions (Legal & Regulatory Framework)					
	Redistribution					
	Land Administration					
	Land Use Planning & Conservation					

N.B. *Individual cells of the table represent critical intersections between land issues being experienced and policy interventions drawn from land programming interventions commonly applied by land tenure practitioners. The severity of issues and the degree of programming intervention can vary in each of these cells depending on the level of donor support, government will, the effectiveness of delivery mechanisms, and the severity of problems experienced in any one country. Finally, issues and efficacy of land reform can be affected and/or informed by the sequencing of these bundles of land reform interventions in each of the cells, and the sequence with which these cells are combined. An illustration of some of the possible programming interventions that can be employed in response to LTPR issues is provided on the following pages, in Table 2.*

Policy and Program Interventions		A Conflict/ Instability	B Insecure Land and Property Rights	C Landlessness/ Inequitable land Distribution	D Poorly Performing Land Markets	E Unsustainable Natural Resource Management
a	Good Governance	Election Reform Restoration of rule of law Reintegration of military Strengthening participation Working on transparency	Public awareness campaigns Decentralization	Resettlement of displaced peoples Strengthening Community Governance Land reform Allocation of state land Resettlement	Public awareness campaigns	Participatory management
b	Conflict or Dispute Resolution	Reconciliation Dispute resolution Formal mediation Arbitration Reintegration Restitution Compensation	Alternative dispute resolution Arbitration Land Court Judiciary reform	Village tribunals		Dispute resolution Agriculture/wildlife conflict Access to protected area resources Local management vs. Commercial exploitation
c	Institutions and Legal and Regulatory Framework	Civil Code Constitutional reform Establishment of Courts Judicial reform Law reform	Land registration Law review commissions Law reform Judicial reform Magistrates Establish notaries Create property institutions Public information campaigns	Law reform Strengthen customary tenure	Law and regulatory reform to enable transactions Mortgaging legislation Legal procedures for recording transactions Review of fee structures	Nat'l Env. Action Plans Protected area legislation Conservation and forestry law reform Licensing
d	Redistribution	Resettlement of soldiers Resettlement of refugees		Refugee settlement Reallocation of state Resettlement Land reform Farm Restructuring Privatization of state assets	Market assisted land reform	Reclassification of land/degraded forest Agrarian reform
e	Land Administration	Land demarcation Land suitability assessments Reconstruction of property Reconstruction of records	Adjudication Land certification Land registration Restitution Registry development Land agency development	Land information systems Geographical information systems Land suitability assessment Land inventory Survey Land demarcation	Cadastral registration Market information Decentralization Valuation Development of real estate professionals Land information Property records	Land information systems Concessions
f	Land Use Planning & Conservation	Land reclamation De-mining Infrastructure rehabilitation		Buffer zone management Protected area mgmt Access to protected areas Co-management	Zoning Taxation Town and regional planning Development incentives	Reforestation Soil conservation Land reclamation Terracing Soil mapping Zoning

3.0 Property Rights and Privatization in Mongolia – Context

3.1 Policy and Legal Framework

The land tenure and property rights framework continues to evolve amidst a political and economic transition in Mongolia that is only 14 years old. With the advent of "privatization" in 1990, land policy and legal framework have received persistent attention. In order to implement the intent of the Constitution, the Civil Code, and the overarching objectives of the Land Law in 1994, the Mongolian government passed Resolution 143 in 1995. The Resolution gave local government units at *soum* and *aimag* levels the primary responsibility for implementation of the Land Law. However, the subsequent change in institutional arrangements governing land law, and its implementation, suggest that land laws in general appear to be poorly understood and irregularly executed. They appear open to interpretation, with clear opportunities for "rent seeking."

Policy and Laws	
Constitution of Mongolia	1992
Civil Code (revised)	1994
1st Land Law	1994
Law on Special Protected Areas	1995
Law on Land Fee Payment	1997
Land Valuation Resolution No. 152	1997
2nd Land Law	2002 – promulgated in 2003
Law on Mongolian Citizen's Ownership of Land	2002 – promulgated in 2003
Land Fees – Resolution No. 103 Valuation and Methodology	2003
Other Related Land Laws	
Law on Subsoil	1989
Forest Code	1995
General Law on Environmental Protection	1995
Law on Registration of Immovable Property	1997
Law on Mineral Rights	1997
Law on Cadastral Survey and Land Cadastre	1999
Law on Immovable Property Tax	2000

A quick summary of provisions for land tenure in Mongolia include:

♦ *Private Ownership (also called ownership rights, title deed/freehold)*. At the present time, only family households can own land, not individuals, though the law in this regard is confusing. Private ownership of agricultural and commercial lands has not yet been granted. Businesses and foreign individuals are not allowed to own land.

♦ *Lease Rights (also called licenses) for possession rights (Mongolians) and use rights (which can apply to Mongolians and foreign interests)*. Lease rights are time-bound and typically include a period of 15-60 years with an option for a 40-year renewal. Mongolian-owned businesses and Mongolia households can hold lease rights. Foreign entities can only obtain use rights. Land use contracts are for five years with one possible extension. They are expressly forbidden from using land for agriculture or livestock.

Pledges and transactions are legal among Mongolian national businesses and organizations.

As of November 2004, the national land use plan specified a total number of hectares available for private ownership. This total represents just less than 0.03 % of the total land area of the country. That land total can be further divided between:

♦ Residential land – total available hectares = 167,925.62
♦ Agricultural land – total available hectares = 346,926.36
♦ Commercial land – total available hectares = not yet specified

As of November 2004, the following property **can not** be owned:

♦ Forests
♦ Pasture and grazing lands
♦ City Centers/Commercial Lands
♦ Water Basins/Points and Sources
♦ Special Needs Areas/Protected Areas

In addition, fines and fees for land (and over land rights) are established in primary laws and not in subsidiary laws or administrative regulations. This system requires a law to be changed in order to change a fee structure, making such changes unwieldy and problematic.

3.2   Land Administration and Management System

Recent GoM restructuring has moved the (Agency) Administration of Land Affairs, Geodesy, and Cartography (ALAGaC) from the Office of the Prime Minister to the newly constituted Ministry of Construction and Urban Development. As part of this move, ALAGaC has been given the mandate to consolidate the functions of (a) national land geodesy and cartography, (b) national land administration and management, and (c) the immovable property registry. As of November 2004, the Agency employed 300 staff nationwide. The newly consolidated Agency has only just started to address its organizational functions and institutional relationships within the Ministry. There is some justifiable concern that the institutional location for the new Agency will marginalize its effectiveness and take away from its more independent and accountable role within government, more broadly. While it is still too early to tell explicitly, there is a measurable degree of confusion over what entity is managing land, land information, coordinating land policy, and conducting land administration.

Since 1995, *soum* and *aimag*-level governments have struggled to fulfill their role regarding land administration, management, and ensuring the security of land rights. A central Land Management Agency was established in 1997 and made provisions for representatives at national, provincial, and district levels. Their roles were to supervise and support the implementation of legislation and regulation of land use. This strategy reflects a strongly decentralized approach to land use planning and management. The *soum* and *aimag* authorities, however, have limited capacity and are insufficiently prepared to implement regulations and enforce elements of the land laws. To date, there is significant evidence to suggest that local government has spent more time on information gathering and zoning than on the allocation of secure land rights. In part, this may stem from insufficient demand for secure land rights; alternatively, it could also stem from a civil service that is largely ill-prepared to accommodate the need and nuance of land laws interpreted at local levels. In addition, severe financial constraints at local government levels make it difficult to attract and retain qualified staff.

3.3   Taxation

The policy and legal framework over land makes provision for taxation. Eighteen (18)-20% of the GOM's revenue is *expected* to come from property tax associated with land. Land valuation and taxation forms a significant part of the new ADB land administration project for the country. The ability, however, to assess and collect this tax at present is negligible, is enforced inconsistently, and is fraught with problems since there is no valuation system yet specified for commercial land. In addition, 90% of the property tax values in the Ger districts of Ulaanbaatar will be exempt from payment for the foreseeable future. This decision is primarily an equity issue and maintains property values at an artificially low level. The decision pushes immovable property as the engine of real economic value and is forming part of the basis for commercial lending. Immovable property drives a new mortgage system and contributes to fundamental economic growth objectives—but it does not include land.

3.4 Government of Mongolia Action Plan

The most recent GoM Action Plan for the country, 2004-2008, is a reflection of government priority and policy. This document has several references to land reform, tenure, and property rights, but those that are important include the following.

Economic Policy – Continue privatization and improve the economic effectiveness of land and private properties:

♦ Intensify land reform and privatization of land to citizens;
♦ Make land ownership and registration information open to the public, and related information access services efficient;
♦ Improve systems to register citizens, real estate, land, and companies;
♦ Move to an integrated coding system of land location (zip code); give value to real estate based on the location code;
♦ Improve the real estate tax;
♦ Differentiate land rental fees based on the productivity and location of land plots;
♦ Implement a policy to expand privatization methods and to improve their efficiency;
♦ Continue privatization of most valued large companies;
♦ Emphasize management privatization in the social sector;
♦ Improve government regulations and transparency in tenders and acquisitions; and
♦ Support irrigated crop farming and privatization of land to farmers.

Under urban planning, development, construction, and land management policies:

♦ Create a unified database on construction, urban planning, land management, land ownership, possession, utilization and assessment, and immovable property; and
♦ Create opportunities for citizens to gain bureaucracy-free access to that information.

Under Rural Infrastructure at regional levels:

♦ Intensify land privatization in rural areas and provide rural populations with opportunity to enjoy economic advantages of land privatization, and private land close to markets and nearby main roads;
♦ Stress attention on land reforms and rural areas and provide general guidelines for regulating land management; and
♦ Promote allocation of land for long-term possession and use to entities specialized in meat and milk production, located close to regional centers, towns, and other populated settlements.

4.0 Property Rights in Mongolia – An Overview of Issues

The USAID team used the "Conceptual Framework" on page 5 to conduct the following analysis and overview of property rights issues in Mongolia. Each of the five major issues characterizing land and property rights reform is addressed here.

Conflict/Instability – No widespread examples of instability or conflict appear to characterize land tenure and land privatization in Mongolia at present. Several examples of conflicts arising over grazing access and grazing rights were cited and, in some cases, resulted in bodily harm and death. In addition, there were several examples of conflict cited over land allocation in the residential "Ger" districts surrounding Ulaanbaatar and Erdinet, most fueled by confusion and manipulation of land use application information, the absence of clear zoning specifications, unclear access, and unclear land rights. Several additional examples were cited over commercial and residential lands in Ulaanbaatar's city center, where disputes regarding citizens' rights over "public and commercial" lands affected city residents and some foreign investors.

The most significant potential areas for future conflicts over land and property rights in Mongolia, however, will be over (1) water and pasture use, access, and rights; (2) equitable and economically viable agricultural land distribution; (3) expansion of protected areas to include customary grazing lands and water resources; and (4) property rights surrounding mining exploration and extraction.

For example, despite Mongolia's progressive reputation for its legal and fiscal approach to the development of its mineral sector, we see the potential for competing and conflicting land rights and property rights to emerge. The Constitution, 1989 Subsoil Law, and 1997 Minerals Law all clearly indicate that the state has exclusive property rights over its mineral resources. There are clearly defined roles and responsibilities for implementing the regulations of this law between Ministries. Provincial and district governments are responsible for organizing and ensuring implementation of mining legislation and compliance with environmental protection, health, and safety regulations at local levels. While there is increasing evidence concerning adverse environmental impacts arising from some mineral extraction, the larger issue remains the inevitable impacts of large-scale mining operations on grazing and water rights and the development of new infrastructure (e.g., labor camps/housing) around mining operations. Unplanned and uncontrolled development of ancillary facilities associated with mining operations could fuel greater conflicts over land access, use, and property rights. Some evidence of similar trends has been experienced along major communication routes with China, to the south.

Landlessness or Inequitable Land Distribution – There are few examples of landlessness in the country. Between May 2003 and May 2005, each Mongolian is officially afforded the opportunity to take up a private, household landholding within their respective "home" areas. The amount of land varies according to the latest land law, with the smallest parcels being granted in large urban areas, and larger parcels being granted in *aimag* and *soum* areas.[3]

Mongolians can obtain use and possession rights (licenses) over land for periods varying from 1-60 years, with the option to renew these for up to another 40 years. Minimum possession rights for 15 years appear to be a result of the new land law. It is unclear as to the degree to which these rights are manipulated by

---

[3] Land privatization in urban areas (approximately 0.02% of total land – but figures vary) is free of payment. Only application fees are paid, and we encountered fee payments that were significantly different than government published rates for different elements of the application. After May 2005, acquisition of land will require payment. Title is only granted to households/families at present. Families in Ulaanbaatar are entitled to 0.07 ha, while in families in rural *aimag* centers and *soum* centers are granted up to 0.35 and 0.5 ha, respectively.

the granting authorities. The amount of land open for privatization is estimated at anywhere between 2-3% of the total land area of Mongolia. At present, approximately 0.03% of the total land area has been privatized, with most of this being in Mongolia's three major urban centers—Ulaanbaatar, Erdinet, and Dahan. Privatization of land in the *aimags* and *soums* is insignificant to date.

To date, there has not been a strong push to acquire private land title outside of the nation's capital, suggesting that there is not a strong interest and most people do not see the need, or that information concerning the opportunity and benefits of private land titling is not widely known. Individuals who possess land on leasehold terms (including farming) and are found within the zones defined as "urban" have the right to purchase it from the state. The degree to which this right is being exercised is unclear. There is some evidence, however, that land allocation (both private and leasehold) remains the domain of the privileged and more affluent of *aimag* and *soum* residents. These consultants were told that this is particularly the case in areas around water sources (for irrigated agriculture), around *soum* and *aimag* centers, and around communication routes.

The most striking case of problematic land distribution appears to be among the more than 100,000 agricultural workers (formerly working on state farms) who do not presently have access to private agricultural land. Agricultural land is not yet privatized, and is not being considered for individual privatization. Instead, agricultural land is expected to be privatized among registered companies.

Insecure Land and Property Rights – These issues are perhaps among the most potentially contentious affecting Mongolians in the immediate future. Government moves toward privatization have been taking place in a considered and cautious fashion. Privatization commenced with livestock in 1993 and was followed by privatization of apartments later in the decade. The 1992 Constitution laid the foundation for the state's right of eminent domain and private land ownership by citizens of Mongolia. The private ownership of pastureland was forbidden, and the Constitution confers the right of fair acquisition, possession, and inheritance of movable and immovable property. It also specified that foreign citizens could not own land. The revised Civil Code of 1994 contains the property law of Mongolia and governs the creation, termination, and transfer of property rights—also making the provision for contract and inheritance law. The Civil Code is also the framework for equal rights possession, use, and disposal of family property. A 1996 amendment allows for mortgage of immovable property, and includes land when it is transferred to private ownership.

The Land Law of 1994 was the first effort of the country to actually regulate possession, use, and protection of land, specifying the rights and obligations of Mongolians related to land rights. Importantly, the Law made provision for the regulation of the use and protection of pasturelands, and the settlement of disputes. It also provided for the possession of rights to state-owned lands (lease and use rights) for Mongolians and foreigners, and specifies their duration.

The most recent set of land laws (the Land Law of 2002 and the Law on Mongolian Citizens' Ownership of Land of 2002, both enacted in 2003) represents an important step forward in land ownership and management of use. Both these laws provide for regulation of transactions related to ownership and use. Specifically, it makes some important improvements to land tenure and rights regarding pasturelands. In addition, the Law on Mongolian Citizens' to Ownership of Land regulates the allocation of land for ownership, types and sizes of land to be owned, as well as indicates the power of local administrations and the procedures for enacting land ownership. Local governments are given the power to appropriate land under state special protection, and the central government possesses the rights to acquire land under possession of citizens, entities, and organizations, for "special needs."

Many of the property rights encompassed within the new laws have yet to be tested (in the courts system or through land markets). Under the new government, there has been additional discussion about opening the issue of individual ownership.

With at least 30% of GDP derived from agriculture and natural resources management affecting between 40 and 50% of the population, property rights remain ambiguous and confusing at best. Land lease rights (group possession rights) and land tenure are at the forefront of different donor agendas that attempt to address land, water, and pasture management, as well as biodiversity conservation and land degradation in rural areas. Property rights are also at issue for Mongolians claiming family land rights within national protected areas, and over forests, wildlife, and non-timber natural resource harvesting. We did not discover any donors dealing with agricultural land reform and agricultural development.

With respect to privatization, private ownership typically involves fewer restrictions on the use and transfer of land, greater security of tenure, and the ability to use land as collateral. Both the Mongolian legislature and the government administration appear focused on issues of equity over economics in the land and property rights discussion. The GOM policy appears to demonstrate concern that privatization will lead to inequitable access to land and conflicts between private and social interests over the use of land. This was particularly evident in discussions with private and community interests over open land/green spaces in Ulaanbaatar. However, it was apparent that the state is managing this process in a "non-transparent" fashion that is undermining their stated goals.

Property rights, however, particularly over land, are emerging through state legislation and private action. Free titling for peri-urban, Ger district dwellers is happening, and for all intents and purposes, could be part of a large-scale urban land management, planning, and private property scheme. However, it was not apparent to the USAID team that there is a well-developed capacity for land use planning in the city, a comprehensive urban management plan for Ulaanbaatar, and how much of these plans are public knowledge. Land titling in the Ger districts can also be interpreted as part of a long-needed move to legitimize "land squatting and land grabbing" that has gone on over the last 14 years, and has intensified since the disastrous affects of the "dzud" on rural transhumance activities between 1999 and 2002.

There is also evidence to suggest that economic linkages are emerging between urban and rural land users/land use—implying economic diversification. There is increasing evidence of families splitting labor between transhumance activities and more sedentary activities focused around commercial centers and small-plot agriculture. This suggests emerging labor markets, agricultural investments (vegetables and forge production) and enterprise diversification (small shops and services). There is also evidence to suggest that land as a "security" and that land as a "market potential" are emerging, often in an adhoc fashion and often outside the scope of the law.

All these property rights importantly are in need of a flexible policy, legal, and regulatory framework that both recognizes and provides a road map for their interpretation and application in an emerging private sector economy—and that fosters private sector investments.

Poorly Performing Land Markets – Given the small amount of land actually at stake in the privatization process, it is no wonder that the official concern of the government appears to be equity over economics. Only limited land privatization has taken place, and only for residential land. This has not yet contributed to privatization goals. The cautious move forward with privation only reinforces the government's emphasis on an "open, fair, and free" process of land acquisition, as a priority between May 2003 and May 2005.

Residential land markets, however, are emerging on a non-formal basis. Evidence was provided to indicate that Ger district land plots were being acquired, bought, and sold. The volume of these transactions is unclear, but this information will become increasingly available as the development of the new land administration agency is realized. A more telling argument, however, is that commercial loan institutions will not yet accept land titles as collateral without donor subsidy. A nascent mortgage market is emerging based on the contents of a "hasha" and not on the land itself. It is also important to recognize that household land privatization under the present legislation will never realize much in the way of income from property taxes for urban, *aimag*, or *soum* budgets. At present, households are 90% exempt from land fees (tax) for family plots up to 0.07 ha.[4]

Privatization of urban real estate (not land) has unleashed a significant amount of wealth and investments (both speculative and productive). Yet land speculation in Ulaanbaatar and its environs (commercial and residential) is occurring without " real costs" and without corresponding land values. To date, there has been no privatization of land designated for commercial purposes. This is scheduled to happen in 2005, and will depend, in large degree, on the adherence to a transparent system of land registration, valuation, and taxation. At the present time, it is unclear as to what degree firms are having trouble securing property rights—the few problem examples encountered did not indicate the severity of the issue. It is our understanding that all commercial property holders (under existing agreements) will be required to buy the land that they possess. The process and regulations that govern this process remain unclear. If land allocation and property rights continue to be allocated and secured in a non-transparent fashion, both speculation as well as real charges of "rent seeking" and serious corruption will persist.

Privatization efforts of agricultural lands are also problematic. The present valuation of agricultural land for privatization is too high for most companies and smallholders to buy land. Most of the agricultural land (formerly some 1.5 m hectares at its most expansive and now less than 400,000 ha.) is currently held by "large companies" under lease arrangements. These same firms are not allowed to hold agricultural land under private land ownership, only individuals can. In addition, these firms must use the land over a three-year period or lose the land and their rights to farm it. The present law does not provide for the sale/transfer of land to individuals.

Land is still not part of a mortgage market. Yet, clearly, the largest incentive for land privatization in both the commercial and large-scale agricultural sectors is to have privatized land serve as one of the engines of economic growth.

Unsustainable Natural Resources Management – This issue is very clearly linked to the security of property rights felt by Mongolians. At present, there are a number of donor-supported efforts focusing on the development of a system(s) of possession rights for pastoralists that balance traditional, communist, and emerging democratic practices in land use management. These models are emerging under the umbrella of pasture management, landscape conservation, and community-based natural resources management projects. As long as economic activity in these areas remains limited, suitable land use alternatives are absent, and environmental risks are high, privatization will have limited application. Instead, group property rights will be central to effective land management and land use systems.

Donor efforts appear spread throughout much of the country. Projects are examining pasture management, wildlife management, and other natural resources management activities built around family and/or customary groups at the *bag* and/or *soum* levels. Lessons are emerging as well as, in particular, examples of how herding "groups" identify and decide to work together in a spirit of "community." New models of collaboration are emerging that suggest a combination of the compulsory collectivism of the "negdel" period and the individualism of the post-communist years.

---

[4] It is also interesting to note that herding households will also be totally exempted from land fee payments for pasture and hay land use.

The equity and resource economics of pastoralism and rural natural resources management and property rights remains in need of a flexible and responsive legislative and regulatory framework that will preserve customary practices, provide economic growth, and encourage sound land use practices. One of the most significant areas for friction remains the expansion of protected areas to include customary grazing lands, thereby exacerbating the institutional conflict among herders, local area authorities, and the Ministry of Nature and the Environment. The potential for institutional rivalry and confusion also surrounds the permitting of "natural resource/natural use" permits, where it is not clear which agency has jurisdiction. One report notes that "a district governor responsible for short-term budgets is unlikely to enforce the implementation of pasture management plans, if these plans limit livestock numbers in a way that would reduce local budget revenues."[5]

---

[5] Land Resources and Their Management, World Bank, Mongolia Environmental Monitor 2003.

5.0 Donor Efforts

Many of the donor efforts in Mongolia have touched upon issues of land reform and privatization. The following table illustrates the consultants' understanding of the present state of donor support addressing issues in land reform and property rights issues in Mongolia.

Table 3   **Donor Programs Addressing Land Reform Issues in Mongolia ***

Donor	Conflict and Instability	Insecure Land and Property Rights	Landlessness/ Inequitable Land Distribution	Poorly Performing Land Markets	Unsustainable Natural Resources Management
ADB		✓		✓	✓
UNDP	✓		✓	✓	✓
Swiss	✓		✓	✓	✓
Dutch			✓	✓	✓
GTZ		✓	✓	✓	✓
USAID				✓	✓
CIDA/IDRC	✓				✓
SIDA	✓			✓	✓

*Any omissions and/or oversights in the table are the fault of the authors. The table should be reviewed and validated by donors as part of their interpretation of the land tenure and property rights conceptual framework presented in this report.

The largest donor investors in land tenure and property rights development are the ADB and GTZ. Both are embarking on new projects to support land management and administration systems, and build capacity within Mongolia's emerging land administration systems. Both are largely focused at the national level, and both are aimed, inevitably, at developing more productive land and property markets. Their efforts are overlapping, and there is reportedly minimal donor coordination on programming matters. Both are implementing their projects through the newly formed (Agency) for Administration of Land Affairs, Geodesy, and Cartography (ALAGaC).

ADB – the ADB is embarking on an $11 million loan and technical assistance projects between 2004 and 2008. Their efforts will focus on a) improvements to the legal and administrative framework for land administration and management; b) cadastral survey work in Ulaanbaatar, Dahan, and Erdinet cities; c) land registration (a National Land Information System); and d) a land valuation and management system aimed at urban land market development.

GTZ – German bilateral assistance is building on a previous seven-year effort in land tenure and national property rights legal reform and administration. They will support a three-year project valued at Euro 2m in support of public education, cadastre development, and unspecified contributions to legal reform and land law. A range management/community-based natural resources management project effort is valued at an additional 1.7m Euro. The geographical focus of this last effort focuses on Gobi *aimags*.

Donor projects addressing various elements of land reform include:

USAID – USAID is addressing some matters related to land reform through three activities that it supports. These include the GOBI Regional Economic Growth Initiative and GER Initiative, where property title is used as collateral against which loans are guaranteed through commercial banks for enterprise development activities. Scale and scope of these are limited. In addition, the USAID is supporting a biodiversity, livelihoods, and landscape conservation project through a Global Conservation

Partnership grant to a U.S.-based NGO for several *aimags* in eastern Mongolia (The Eastern Steppe Living Landscape – Sustaining Wildlife and Traditional Livelihoods in the Arid Grasslands of Mongolia).

More importantly, USAID's largest portfolio of support is for the Economic Policy Reform and Competitiveness Project. Its primary purpose is to accelerate and broaden sustainable, private sector-led economic growth through an improved enabling environment for private sector growth and more competitive industries and sectors. A large part of the Project's strategy focuses on policy analysis, formulation, and implementation support to the Mongolian leadership and administration. In addition, efforts are aimed at consensus building, public education, and national dialogue as well as cluster development and support. It is clear that any additional USAID support for land privatization, including policy development, legal reform, a realistic regulatory framework, and education and training, should be closely coordinated with this major USAID activity.

SDC – The Swiss Agency for Development and Cooperation – Swiss engagement in property rights is a result of focusing support for disaster management and social security as well as integrated crop and livestock production. A new project, entitled 'Green Gold' is focusing their livestock improvement and pasture management interventions in three *aimags*, covering three "eco-zones" in Mongolia. Their annual programming support to this project is valued at $500,000/year, with this first phase operating between 2004 and 2008.

UNDP – The United Nations Development Program – UNDP is implementing a similar suite of projects that are focused on protected areas conservation/biodiversity conservation, disaster management, and grasslands management. Indicating a strong community-based natural resources management approach, the UNDP is operating in concert with the Dutch and GEF in four *aimags* in western Mongolia—a landscape conservation project that is focused on property rights and forestry, wildlife/hunting, and non-timber forest products. World Vision is providing training and facilitation services to this effort. With FAO, UNDP is working on a CBNRM forestry project focused on developing policy and practice. This effort is 1.5 years in duration (2004-2005) and is focused as well on adding value to natural products and the diversification of rural enterprise opportunities.

UNDP is also implementing a community-based natural resources management project focused in three *aimags*, focusing on four *soums* in each. Their efforts focus on a combination of range management, livestock management alternatives (comparing different eco-zones), veterinary services, and livestock improvement. This project is 1.5 years old in a project cycle that began in 2003 and ends in 2006. Expenditures are approximately $600K/year.

Most recently, UNDP has undertaken to consolidate the experiences of the Germans, Swiss, EU/TACIS, WWF, and relevant Ministries in a conference, the outputs of which will be used to inform the new land law. This conference took place on December 15 and 16, 2004, in Ulaanbaatar.

Dutch – Dutch bilateral aid is administered through the UNDP and GTZ. They are supporting pasture management, natural resources management, and property rights efforts. The amount of their support is unknown.

SIDA – The Swedish Development Agency is reportedly supporting pasture management activities on an experimental basis in Hovd Aimag. The amount and duration of their support is unknown.

CIDA/IDRC – the Canadian International Development Agency, through the International Development and Research Council is supporting pasture management activities in three *aimags*. The value and the duration of their support are unknown.

6.0   Challenges and Recommendations

Despite an abundance of donor attention to elements of land and property rights reform, and in addition to one of the highest per capita levels of donor assistance in the world, privatization and property rights are still some time away from becoming an engine for economic growth in Mongolia. In addition, donors, despite their best intentions, continue to focus more on the mechanics of land administration and management than on the creation of secure property rights as a tool in a national economic development agenda. There is a real need to nurture a more rigorous cycle of policy development, legislative reform, realistic, experience-based regulations, and feedback mechanisms that are used to re-inform policy and institutional development. Among the most significant of Mongolia's challenges are the following.

Poorly functioning land markets - With commercial and agricultural land privatization still outstanding, it is too early to say how these privatization efforts will contribute to strengthened land markets, income generation, revenue generation, and economic growth. Experience in the FSU suggests that while these programs are being designed and implemented, it is essential to identify clear privatization objectives and to describe indicators that will be followed and measured to indicate impact. In addition, experience with privatization must be collected and analyzed by a forum (or series of forums) that include government and civil society (and supported by donors). This dialog and critical analysis must be used to inform policy, legislative development, and a realistic regulatory framework in support of additional efforts.

Public access to information – Access to public information on land reform and property rights remains a significant challenge to Mongolia's emerging attempts with privatization. We encountered misunderstanding and confusion over land legislation and the roles of implementing agencies. We saw little evidence of public engagement in national land legislation and no evidence of public consultation in the development of the new land legislation. Newly elected legislators with whom we met were largely without any understanding of land law and its implementation.

Pasture use and possession rights – Common pool resource rights will remain a significant challenge to present and future administrations. The GoM will continue to struggle with how to accommodate implementation of pasture and other common property resource rights under the new land law, and/or decide if these issues must be dealt with under new legislation. A more engaging and informative forum for the development, testing, dialog, and sharing of experiences on these types of property rights reform must be created if the wide variety of donor interventions are to have any meaningful contributions to national policy on this subject.

Property rights and poverty alleviation – The concept of poverty in Mongolia is an elusive one in the context of a pastoralist economy among seemingly endless grazing resources. However, privatization, property rights, and poverty alleviation will continue to plague the development of new policy and legislation as long as there are only limited mechanisms to translate lessons learned and best practices into serious improvements in land management and sustainable economic growth. For example, several donor organizations are working to address viable alternatives to herding. In addition, there is increasing evidence that there is a very significant move towards absentee herd owners and greater human migration to urban centers. The impact of these trends needs to be addressed in both rural and urban arenas, and the impact of these trends relative to property rights and privatization examined.

7.0 The Role of USAID

USAID plays a preeminent role in the development of land tenure policy and property rights worldwide. USAID/Mongolia is uniquely placed to help the GoM and to galvanize and better coordinate donor efforts in land privatization. To further the aims of its economic growth and good governance objectives, USAID/Mongolia should engage in a two-phased approach to address these issues. In the first phase, lasting approximately 1-1.5 years, USAID should focus on land and property rights policy development, a legal framework coupled with realistic regulatory tools, and land and natural resource tenure education and training. At the end of this first phase, USAID will have both a clearly defined exit strategy and a clear set of options for pursuing additional reform efforts in a second phase.

Phase 1

A three-person team, with intermittent engagement in Mongolia, could implement the following activities, coordinated through an existing USAID activity already operating in the country.

Activity 1: Legal Reform

Provide direct legal technical assistance to the GoM to examine all aspects of existing property laws, and to identify and prioritize legal gaps, opportunities, and specific legislative needs required to develop and implement a more comprehensive and clear private property rights system.

Illustrative activities include review of existing legislation, review of existing donor support to land reform legislation and policy development in Mongolia, review of legislative drafting and public review procedures, review and analysis of best land reform practices in the region, and a review of sequencing of land reforms in the Mongolian context.

Output – A comprehensive review of the legal framework, needs and opportunities, best practices, and priorities for legislative reform and policy development from other FSU countries.

Activity 2: Draft Legislation and Form Bipartisan Support

For these changes, based on the priorities arising from Phase 1, the legal team will undertake two key tasks. First, the legal team will draft and submit for consideration priority legislation (laws, amendments, regulations, etc.) for review by government. Second, it will work with key Legislative Committees (Land, Agriculture, Natural Resources, Finance, Office of the Prime Minister, Office of Speaker, etc.) and other GoM agencies to identify and develop bi-partisan support for land policy dialog and legal reform. This focal group will spearhead land reform policy and legislation.

Output – (1) legislation (laws, amendments, regulations) for gaps identified and priority themes and issues derived from Phase 1, and (2) Formation of a bi-partisan constituency and forums that will champion and guide land reform policy and legislation.

Activity 3: Land and Natural Resources Tenure Education and Training

In order to improve the dialog and development of land and property rights policy, there is an important need to provide legislators and government administrators with basic concepts and information on land tenure and property rights. These officials should be assisted to develop an understanding of how these impact economic growth, good governance, and natural resources management. This effort will provide information and best practices identified in Activity 1, to a limited constituency, as identified in Activity 2.

Outputs – Key constituents will be educated on best practices in land and property rights reform in the former Soviet Union, and the impacts of land privatization on economic growth and governance in Mongolia.

Activity 4: Design Follow-on Activities for USAID/Mongolia

There is a need for programming that will further deepen the land privatization process. Activities could include work with/on local/national cadastre, land valuation and taxation, legal training (including the development of a bench book on property law), facilitation of the privatization of commercial and agricultural land, and property rights for rural producers.

Outputs – Design recommendations for USAID/Mongolia project activities.

Appendix 1: Schedule of Meetings – Ulaanbaatar, Mongolia

Date	Organization
16/11/2004	USAID – Mongolia Office
16/11	USAID – Economic Policy Reform and Competitiveness Project
16/11	USAID – Ger Initiative
17/11	USAID – GOBI Regional Economic Growth Initiative
17/11	US Embassy - Commerce and Economic Office
17/11	USAID – Judicial Reform Project
17/11	GTZ – Land Administration Project
17/11	Khann Bank
18/11	ADB – Telecon with ADB former Country Officer for land and land reform, D. Teeter
18/11	ADB – Capacity Building for Cadastral Survey and Land Registration Project
18/11	The Asia Foundation
18/11	Mongolia Ministry of Industry and Trade – Head of Department of Geology and Mining
18/11	Trade and Development Bank
19/11	Ivanhoe Mines
19/11	Ministry of Agriculture and Food, Head of Crops Sector Department
19/11	Administration of Land Affairs, Geodesy and Cartography
19/11	Movement for the Fair Privatization of Land and the Foundation for Agricultural Development
22/11	Center for Policy Research
22/11	Open Society Forum
22/11	Ulaanbaatar City Office for Land
22/11	Meeting with an advisor to the Prime Minister and former head of the Liberty Center
23/11	United Nations Development Program
23/11	GTZ advance team for
24/11	Swiss Agency for Development and Cooperation
N.B.	*Attempts were made to gather information from the World Bank office in Beijing, but Bank offices were closed for a significant period of time during this assessment.*

Appendix 2: Mongolia Reference List

1. Action Plan for the Government of Mongolia, 2004-2008. English Translation, Chemonics-International, EPRC Project, Ulaanbaatar, Mongolia.

2. Baas, S., Batjargal, E., Swift, J., (2001), Pastoral Risk Management for Disaster Prevention and Preparedness in Central Asia with Special Reference to the Case of Mongolia, Asia-Pacific Conference on Early Warning, Prevention Preparedness and Management of Disasters in Food and Agriculture, Changmai, Thailand, FAO.

3. Dialog between Cultures and Civilizations: Present State and Perspectives of Nomadism in a Globalizing World," International Conference, (Abstracts of Papers and Poster Presentations), Jorg-Janzen, Dr., Editor, (2004).

4. Enkh-Amgalan, A., (1997), Summary of the Final Report on Land Reform, Strategic Support for Economic and Social Growth, MON/97/131, Government of Mongolia.

5. Fernandez-Gimenez, Maria E, (2002), Spatial and Social Boundaries and the Paradox of Pastoral Land Tenure: A Case Study from Post-socialist Mongolia, *Human Ecology*, Vol. 30, No.1, March.

6. Fernandez-Gimenez, Maria E. and B. Batbuyan, (2004), Law and Disorder: Local Implementation of Mongolia's Land Law, Development and Change 35(1): 141-165

7. Finch, C., (2003), Mongolia Conflict Vulnerability Analysis, Background Paper No. 5 in preparation for the USAID/Mongolia 2004-2008 Country Strategy.

8. Finch, c., (2003), Mongolia Environment Analysis, Background Paper No. 2 in preparation for the USAID/Mongolia 2004-2008 Country Strategy.

9. GTZ, Law and Economics, Reforms Shape Mongolia's Future, Advisory Service to Legal Reform in Mongolia (2003).

10. Hanstad, T., Duncan, J., (2001), Land Reform in Mongolia: Observations and Recommendations, RDI Reports on Foreign Aid and Development #109, Seattle, Washington, for the World Bank.

11. Keith, Simon (2004), Land Management and Valuation Report, ADB Mongolia Capacity Building for Cadastral Survey and Land Registration, (TA 3395)-MON.

12. Law on Allocation of Land to Mongolian Citizens for Ownership, (2002) Government of Mongolia, Ulaanbaatar.

13. Law of Mongolia on Land, (2003), Government of Mongolia, Ulaanbaatar.

14. McEwen, A., (2003), Capacity Building for Cadastral Survey and Land Registration TA 3395-MON, ADB Contract No. COCS/03-581, On the Implementation of the Land Law and Land Privatization Law, Ulaanbaatar, Mongolia.

15. Mearns, Robin, (2004), Decentralization, Rural Livelihoods and Pasture-Land Management in Post-Socialist Mongolia, *European Journal of Development Research*, Vol. 16, No.1, pp.133-153.

16. Morton, J., Amgaa, S., and Enkhbat, A., (2002), Evaluation of a Pilot Project with Herders' Groups, A Report to UNDP Mongolia and the Netherlands Ministry of Foreign Affairs.

17. Republic of Mongolia - Medium-term Concept Paper, Mongolia (2003-2005), SDC, Ulaanbaatar, Mongolia.

18. Singer, Norman J., Report on the Law of Mongolia on Land and the Law of Mongolia on Land Fees, (2001), for the Economic Policy Support Project, USAID – Mongolia.

19. Singer, Norman J., (2002) Review of Law on Allocation of Land to Mongolian Citizens for Ownership, for the Economic Policy Support Project, USAID – Mongolia.

20. Swiss Agency for Development and Cooperation, Green Gold Pasture Management Program (2004), Ulaanbaatar, Mongolia.

21. USAID/Mongolia, Strategic Plan, (2004-2008), Ulaanbaatar, Mongolia, 2003.

22. World Bank, (2003), Mongolia, Land Resources and their Management, Ulaanbaatar, Mongolia.

www.ingramcontent.com/pod-product-compliance
Lightning Source LLC
Chambersburg PA
CBHW081432310526
45790CB00020B/3728